LONDON :

SUTTON SHARPE AND CO., PRINTERS, 145, QUEEN VICTORIA STREET, E.C.

PREFACE.

WE desire to call the attention of our customers, and of the trade generally, to one of the most recent of the many attempts which have been made to disparage our manufacture. The following pages contain a report slightly condensed from the *Freeman's Journal* of the 30th of November and of the 2nd of December, and compared with the reports given in *Ridley's Circular* and in the *Wine Trade Review* of an action for libel brought by us against the Dublin Whisky Distillery, Limited, in which the jury awarded to us £100 damages, although we had sustained no actual pecuniary loss, but manifestly as an expression of opinion with regard to the nature of the course which had been pursued by the defendants. Our action against a Mr. Godsell, the London agent of the defendant Company, who had distributed some of the circulars in which the libel was contained, had previously been tried in the English Court of Queen's Bench, and a verdict in our favour, with 40s. damages, had been followed by a judicial award of costs. It is worthy of note that the defendants, as will be seen in the report of the evidence, had attempted to set up for themselves a reputation for using none but Irish grain in their manufacture. Such a course might by some be regarded as patriotic—although the truest patriotism would undoubtedly be to give the distinctively Irish product the benefit of being made from the best grain obtainable in the markets of the world. In this respect, as it turned out, the practice of the defendants was better than their professions, for their Manager, who in the course of the London trial swore that his Company never used foreign grain, had found occasion to refresh his memory upon the point before the trial of the second action in Dublin, and there confessed to the use of foreign grain, the purchase of which he had previously "forgotten." We place the whole story upon record in this permanent form because it seems to point to the introduction into commerce of practices of an entirely new description. A few years ago no respectable manufacturer, or even salesman, would have attempted to secure business by casting unfounded aspersions upon well-established competitors; and it is high time that dealers should be made acquainted with this novel method of endeavouring to obtain orders, and should be on their guard against being deceived by it. We feel that our best protection against any who libel our manufacture will be the genuine experience of its quality which purchasers may easily acquire for themselves, together with the love of truthfulness and of fair play to which we appeal by the issue of this pamphlet.

GEORGE ROE & COMPANY.

THE DUBLIN WHISKY TRADE.

——⟨◊⟩——

IN the Court of Common Pleas on November 29th, before
Chief Justice Morris and a city special jury, the hearing of
the case of Roe *v.* The Dublin Whisky Distillery Company
(Limited) was commenced. The action was brought by Mr.
Henry Roe, D.L., trading as a distiller under the name of
George Roe and Co., to recover damages laid at £10,000,
for an alleged libel contained in a circular published by the
directors of the Dublin Whisky Company (Limited),
Jones' Road.

Counsel for the plaintiff: Messrs. D. C. Heron, Q.C.;
James Murphy, Q.C., and John Atkinson, instructed by
Messrs. D. and T. Fitzgerald. Counsel for the defendants:
Messrs. F. Macdonogh, Q.C.; R. P. Carton, Q.C., and W.
Kenny, instructed by Messrs. Larkin and Co.

Mr. Atkinson opened the pleadings. The summons and
plaint contained several counts, in the first of which the
plaintiff complained that he is a distiller under the name of
George Roe and Co., and makes and distils old still Whisky
from barley of the best description; that during the season of
1877, and before the next, he fixed the price at the opening of
the season and announced it to his customers; and he complained that the defendants maliciously published the following
circular:—

Dublin Whisky Distillery Company.
Old Still Distillers. No patent still on their premises.
Distillery, Jones' Road, October 27th, 1877.

DEAR SIR,—I am instructed to acquaint you that the directors of
this company have fixed their opening price for new whisky in the
season first commencing at 4s. 1d. per gallon, 25 o.p., free on board in
Dublin with same allowances at last season for cash, casks, and quantity.
From the price temporarily quoted by one of our Dublin distillers it be-
comes necessary for us to explain, on this occasion, to our customers that
the increase of 2d. per gallon in our opening price for this season has been
rendered unavoidable by the increased price of the class of grain used in
our manufacture. No doubt old still whisky can be made from foreign
barleys or from damaged native grain at the prices of last season, or even
less, but for the class of whisky to which the success of this Company is

indebted, and which the Directors are determined to maintain at any cost, none but barleys of the best quality can be used. A reference to any of our market notes will show what high prices such barleys command this season. We trust that our friends and customers will realise the fact that the increase we announce to-day is a moderate one, and only about one-half that which might be fairly based on the present prices of first-class grain in the markets.

Yours, &c.,
GEORGE S. SOUL,
Secretary.

To that the defendants pleaded several defences. First, they denied the publication; secondly, the defamatory sense; thirdly, they alleged that they did not publish it of or concerning the plaintiff; and, fourthly, that it was no libel. There were two special defences—the first being that the plaintiff and the defendant manufactured old still whisky, and that the defendants had fixed their price at 4s. 2d., per gallon, and that the plaintiff had announced his at 4s.1d.; that they had heard that the plaintiff had purchased large quantities of foreign barley, and that they had an interest in communicating to their customers the reason for the increase in the price of their own commodity, and that they published the circular *bona fide* and without malice. The second special defence averred as a fact that the plaintiff had purchased the foreign barley.

Mr. Heron, Q.C., stated the case for the plaintiff, Mr. Henry Roe, who, he said, complained of a libel published by the defendants in reference to him and his trade, which made it absolutely imperative on him to bring this action for the purpose of protecting his own property and trade, and that of his customers. The defendants were the Dublin Whisky Distillery Company, who had been carrying on business as distillers at Jones' Road since 1872—a most respectable company, against whose manufacture of the best of Whisky Mr. Roe did not instruct him to say a single word. For a hundred years the house of George Roe and Co. had maintained their character for fair dealing, honest manufacture, and friendly dealing with all engaged in the trade, whether as rivals or as customers. This libel was published under circumstances peculiarly injurious, and accompanied by conduct on the part of the defendants and their servants, which was calculated to injure the best established house either in England or Ireland. There were in Dublin until recently four principal distillers: John Jameson, Power, William Jameson, and Roe. Recently there had been added the defendants; and another company. It was the practice in autumn for the distillers to announce their prices for new Whisky. Shortly before 20th October, 1877, Mr. Roe fixed the new spirit at 4s. 1d. per gallon, or a penny off for cash, the traders supplying their own casks; and this price became immediately known—among others to Mr. Costello, the manager of the Dublin Whisky Distillery Company, who, counsel believed, composed this libel; to their secretary, Mr. Soul, who had been for five or six years in the employment of Messrs. George Roe and Co., and to Mr. Valentine Grady, their town traveler. Mr. Grady, in addition to being town traveller for the defendants, occupied also the very important position in being author of the trade article in the *Freeman's Journal*—a most important position. In London they all knew that the parties who had the privilege of writing the trade articles for the *Times* or the *Telegraph* had the most tremendous power of making or marring the fortunes of companies, and though our transactions in Dublin were smaller, still the authors of commercial articles had very great power, and it certainly appeared a most extraordinary thing that, by a fortuitous concurrence of intellect and employment, the town traveler of the defendants was the author of the commercial articles in the *Freeman's Journal*. A few days before the 20th October, Mr. Harris, the manager of the plaintiff, had informed Mr. Grady that he was going to continue the prices of last season. On Monday, the 22nd October, Grady published this article in the *Freeman's Journal*, which Costello stated that he read that morning:—

Whisky.—The market continues fairly firm, and a steady business was done by private hand this week in most of our Dublin brands. In W. J. and Co.'s make there has been much activity. The announcement of Messrs. Roe's present present price for new Whisky came to us so late last week that we had no time to express our opinion upon it. At first it took us by surprise, as it did the entire trade but on reflection the word "present" seems to imply that the price is a temporary one, and we are informed that this is really so, and has reference merely to a few contracts which Messrs. Roe had undertaken at last season's prices. The price under the circumstances cannot, therefore, be regarded as Messrs. Roe's season price. Neither at John's Lane, Marrowbone Lane, nor Jones' Road, have they as yet fixed a price, but at the latter we understand they have decided on advancing their price.

Counsel presumed the Freeman's Journal never knew that any man connected so directly with the trade as a town traveller for a Dublin house was the person privileged to give his opinion of commercial matters as the impartial, editorial "We." However, the drift of this article was obvious. It was read by Mr. Costello on the morning of the 22nd October, and on that day he told Mr. Soul, quite privately, to get a sample of Roe's new Whisky. Those samples were usually openly asked for and freely given, and out of the two million of gallons manufactured by Mr. Roe that year, with the exception of the sample which ultimately found its way into the defendants' hands, there was not an ounce of bad or tainted Whisky. But Mr. Costello did not take the proper course, if he wanted a fair sample, of sending his compliments to Mr. Roe for one. If he had done so the transaction they were now investigating would, probably, never have occurred. Instead of that, Soul instructed Grady, the town traveler, to get a sample. He applied, not to Mr. Roe, but to Mr. Reynolds, the manager of the house of Seely and Co.; and Mr. Reynolds applied to Mr. Harris, the plaintiff's manager for a sample. That sample was in the hands of Costello and Soul before the circular was published, and was perfectly we-known to be a foul and unmerchantable sample, and not a fair sample of Roe's manufacture; yet that foul and unmerchantable sample was exhibited in Dublin and in London by the defendants as Roe's Whisky. It would be part of the present inquiry how did the accident happen to the two or three ounces of Whisky given to the defendants alone, out of the two million gallons manufactured that season, every gallon of which was sold, and no single customer ever complained of. The property that might be injured by this course of conduct was of the most startling magnitude. At the time of the pub-lication of this libel, there was sold by Mr. Roe, and stored by traders in Dublin, Whisky of the value of at least one million, which, by the conduct of the defendants, might have been depreciated to the most startling extent in the hands of those customers. Counsel then proceeded to read the circular com-plained of as a libel, contending that it could only have refer-ence to the plaintiff, who was the only distiller who had then published his price, that its reference to the temporary character of the price was plainly the echo of the opinion expressed in the commercial article in the *Freeman*, and that the innuendo conveyed by the circular was that Mr. Roe used damaged native grain in his manufacture. Mr. Courtney had been the London agent of the defendants. He retired, and was suc-ceded by Mr. Frederick Godsell. Counsel read letters from Mr. Soul, enclosing copies of the circular to Mr. Godsell. There was a custom in the trade in London that traders gave a conditional order, which they might cancel if they did not like the season's prices when they came out. This was referred to in one of Mr. Soul's letters, in which he made arrangements to meet the contingency of orders being withdrawn on the announcement of the defendants' price for the season. It would be proved that for any quantity above 25 butts Roe's price was a penny per gallon dearer than the defendants', and the smaller quantities were precisely the same price, because the defendants took off a penny for the casks, a penny for cash, and a penny for quantity, and Mr. Roe only took off a penny for cash, and nothing for either casks or quantity, so that when they were considering the *bona fides* of Mr. Costello in writing that no doubt old still Whisky might have been made at the price of last season from foreign barley, or from damaged native grain, the jury would ask themselves what was the meaning of that allusion, except either deception on the general public, who might not be perfectly familiar with the details of the trade, or else mere abuse of Roe's Whisky, most seriously affecting his trade and his character. He submitted that this fact was conclusive, that there was no real or *bona fide* motive in the publication, except the desire to injure a rival trader. Upon the 31st October, after two meetings of the directors of the defendants' company in Dublin, Mr. Soul wrote to Mr. Godsell, "I send you this day sample of George Roe and Co.'s Whisky, so that you may compare it with ours." That is, this sample which was known to be foul and unmerchantable was sent to London for the purpose of being shown to Mr. Roe's customers, and, if possible, of destroying his trade. An attempt was made in an action against Mr. Godsell, tried in London, to say that this sample was only sent for the purpose of satisfying Godsell's own mind, and that he alone was to compare Roe's sample with their own; but Costello himself stated that the directors did not restrict Godsell as to the use of it. Counsel characterized this as being as unmercantile a transaction as ever was disclosed before a jury. He went through the defence, which he termed a rigmarole one, omitting a part of Hamlet by omitting any justification of the words "or damaged native grain." On the 12th November, complaint having been made of the libel, Mr. Soul wrote to Mr. Roe that he had brought his letter before the directors, and "was instructed to say that the directors regretted to notice that Mr. Roe considered that a libel upon him was conveyed in their circular, as they failed to see there was any such contained therein. If this explanation was not sufficient, their solicitors were Messrs. Larkin and Co., whose services they hoped, after this explanation, would not be required." After the service of the plaint on the 29th November, Mr. Soul wrote a private letter to Mr. Roe, in which he said: "I have laid before the directors of this company a copy of the summons and plaint in the above action. They find now that the only cause of complaint put forward by you is the reference in the circular to damaged native grain. I am instructed to state that the directors entirely repudiate and disclaim any desire to attribute to you, whether by innuendo or otherwise, the use of damaged grain in the manufacture of your Whisky; and, after a careful examination of the circular, they cannot bring themselves to think it is fairly susceptible of any such interpretation. They authorize me to express their very great regret that you should have considered their reference to damaged native grain applied to the Whisky manufactured by you." Counsel submitted that this private letter was no apology for having publicly circulated all over the world, by this circular and by the exhibition of a foul and unmerchantable sample, that Mr. Roe was making Whisky of damaged native grain. He trusted the verdict of the jury would establish that one rival could never get the business of another by calumny and slander.

Mr. Soul, examined by Mr. James Murphy, Q.C.: Witness said he was secretary in the establishment of the defendants. Whitness had occupied that position since 1872, having been for five or six years before that in Mr. Roe's office. (Circular handed to witness.) Witness drew the MS. of the circular by Mr. Costello's direction. Mr. Costello drew up the original draft. The draft was destroyed, as was also witness's copy, as soon as the circular was in print. Witness could not distinctly recollect whether Mr. Costello amended the original draft in witness's presence. Witness could not swear whether the original draft first seen by witness contained the words "damaged native grain." The words "foreign barley" were in it. Witness could not say whether the draft was interpolated or amended under advice. Witness was at the board after the circular was in print. So far as witness could recollect he first saw the draft on the 17th of October. The price was announced on the 15th October. Costello brought witness the draft. There was a printed copy of the circular before the Board on the 20th. Nothing was said about getting a sample of Roe's Whiskey. Some of the circulars were addressed for agents in Liverpool, Glasgow, Greenock. There were about 5,000 of them printed. The sample of Roe's Whisky was before the Board on the 20th. It was considered not to be up to Roe's standard. There was a peculiarity about it. Witness was not aware that it was ever said that it would show well beside that of the Dublin Whisky Distillery Company. Mr. Costello told me about the 20th to get a sample. Witness got it on the 26th or 27th for Mr. Grady. Witness had asked Mr. Grady on the 26th to get it. At the time of the printing of this circular no other distiller in Dublin to witness's knowledge published his price. There was no sample of the Whisky of any other Dublin distiller in the Dublin Whisky Distillery Company's office. There was no other whose price was then out.

Cross-examined by Mr. Carton, Q.C.: The Dublin Whisky Distillery Company's price in October '76, was 4s., with the same allowance as in '77; in '75 the price was 3s. 9d. The company did not commence manufacturing Whisky until July, '73. In '73 the price was 4s. 6d. The company has been using the best class of barley to be had—native barley, with the exception of one or two exceptional cases. There was a difference of 2s. a barrel in the price of barley in '77 as compared with the price in '76. The season was wet. That increase in price would represent 3d. to 4d. a gallon difference in price of the Whisky. The company take their water from the canal—from the same level as that of John Jameson's.

Re-examined by Mr. Murphy: There is kept in the establishment what is called the corn ledger, giving all the prices and quantities purchased.

Mr. Henry Roe, examined by Mr. Heron, Q.C.: The distillery of George Roe and Co. had been in witness's family for about 100 years. In the season 1877 witness bought barley as low as 17s. 6d., and up to 20s. It was of the best quality. Witness was the first of the Dublin distillers to announce his price. The others had not begun to work. Witness did not employ in the manufacture of Whisky, intentionally, any damaged native grain. They used about 200,000 barrels of barley. That would manufacture about two millions of gallons. All that was sold. There was no complaint in reference to any of it. They were very rarely asked for samples. Selling by sample was not the course of business with known established houses. The Whisky of that year's manufacture had gone up to 5s. 3d. and 5s. 6d., and it went back again to about 5s. There was a heaviness in the trade which rendered it impossible to state the price to a penny. Witness read the circular of the Dublin Whisky Distillery Company. The words, "the price temporarily quoted by one of the Dublin distillers," could only refer to himself; there was no one else at work—no one had made a price. He believed the words, "no doubt old still Whisky can be made from foreign or from damaged native grain at the prices of last season, or even less," were intended to apply to him. He had always used foreign barley. It was used by the other first-class distillers in Dublin. Provided the foreign barley was judiciously chosen, there was not the slightest difference in the article produced; but there was greater difficulty in the mashing. There was more gluten and less starch in the foreign barley, and this caused the difficulty in mashing. They rarely looked abroad for barley if they could get it at home. There was not enough grown at home to supply them. If they were to depend on the supply from home growth alone they would raise the price 5s. or 6s. per barrel. On the 27th October there would have been about 1,200 or 1,300 puncheons of that season's Whisky purchased and in bond. That represented about £22 a puncheon. The brew-ings are called "periods." During the season of 1877 all the "periods" were of a uniform character, and were up to the usual standard.

Cross-examined by Mr. Monroe, Q.C.: All their Whisky was sold that season, and they could have sold more. They had to carry over 2,000 gallons to next season. They had used about 100,000 barrels of foreign grain, at prices from 17s. 6d. to £1.

Robert Harris, manager of Mr. Roe's distillery, deposed that customers of Mr. Roe's spoke to him about the circulars issued by the Dublin Whisky Distillery Company. There was no difference in the quality of Messrs. Roe's Whisky in 1877. Witness gave Mr. Reynolds two samples of Whisky, and some time after Mr. Reynolds brought back one of the samples. It had a musty smell, and was not at all like the ordinary Whisky of Roe's manufacture.

Cross-examined by Mr. Carton: When the sample was got back from Reynolds witness threw it out.

To Mr. Atkinson: It was in the original bottle, but both Mr. Reynolds and witness agreed that it was not Roe's Whisky.

Mr. E. J. Figgis, commission agent and English agent for Mr. Roe, deposed that the Whisky of 1877 was not at all inferior to that of preceding years. There was no peculiarity of taste or smell. The circular was sent to witness by one of our largest customers in England—Liverpool. The average purchase by that customer from Mr. Roe was from 400 to 600 puncheons.

Did he make any complaint?

Mr. Carton objected.

Chief Justice Morris said it might be concluded that he did not order 600 puncheons additional (laughter). There were some things too obvious to prevent conclusions being drawn from them. The laws of evidence were strict, but the laws of common sense are obvious.

Witness continued to say that he was aware that large quantities of foreign barley were used by Dublin distillers.

John Steen, operative distiller in Mr. Roe's establishment, deposed that the Whisky manufactured from foreign barley was as good as that from native barley, provided the foreign barley was of good quality. Witness saw the sample returned by Mr. Reynolds to Mr. Harris. It was empty. It seemed to have been reduced with dirty water. It was perfectly unmerchant-able Whisky.

Cross-examined by Mr. Carton: About one-third or one-fourth of the barley is malted, and the rest is used in the raw state. The barley use is about one-third foreign and two-thirds native.

Mr. Allingham, spirit merchant, Capel Street, and Mr. Devine were examined, and deposed that they understood the reference in the circular to be to Messrs. Roe's Whisky.

Patrick Brannigan, keeper of the spirit store in Messrs. Roe's, deposed as to the method of preparing sample bottles. The bottles were first cleansed with water and then with Whisky, and that is thrown out before the sample is put in.

Chief Justice Morris: A very artistic operation.

William Reynolds deposed that he was in the employment of Messrs. Seely and Co. On the 20th October Mr. Grady asked witness to get a sample of Roe's Whisky for Mr. Costello. Witness got two samples. They were put in a sample case, which was not locked, and there were workmen about. They remained in the case for four or five days, when witness gave Mr. Grady one of the bottles. Five or six weeks after Mr. Grady asked witness if he could get him a sample the exact same as the previous one. Witness asked him what he wanted it for, and he said to send to London—that the other had been sent to London. Witness refused, and said if he had known that the other was to be sent to London he would not have given it to him. Witness, after Mr. Grady left, tested the other sample and it was faulty—it had a musty flavour. In consequence of what had occurred, witness tasted the 1877 Whisky of Roe's make, which Messrs. Seely had in bond, and it was like what Roe's Whisky usually was—up to the usual standard—quite unlike the sample.

James Tyrrell, dealer in grain, deposed that he had not sold any foreign barley, except a small quantity, to the Dublin Whisky Distillery Company. In the present year, 1878, witness sold a quantity to John Jameson and Sons.

Mr. Charles Thomas Sutton, manager for the firm of Sutton, Cardin and Co., rectifying distillers, London, deposed to having seen Mr. Godsell last year, and been shown samples by him at witness's distillery.

Mr. Carton objected.

Mr. Heron said Mr. Godsell was the agent of the Dublin Whisky Distillery Company.

Mr. Carton: It was one thing to be an agent, and another thing for the Company to be responsible for anything Mr. Godsell might do.

Chief Justice Morris: The sample was sent to Mr. Godsell, and it could not be, he presumed, to drink it.

Witness: Mr. Godsell said they would be greatly disappointed in Mr. Roe's Whisky of the season. He brought a sample and it was tested, and they agreed that it was musty. Witness's firm got 100 butts of Messrs. Roe's Whisky that year, and it was as good as usual.

Cross-examined by Mr. Carton: Our firm are rectifying distillers. We buy spirit from London distillers—that is, a neutral spirit, and it is coloured and called gin. We sell George Roe's Whisky as we get it.

Mr. Norton, of the firm of Barry, Norton and Co., deposed to having sold foreign barley to Messrs. Roe, Wm. Jameson, and John Power and Son. He had sold foreign wheat to Messrs. John Jameson and Son, but he did not recollect having sold them any foreign barley.

The letters having been handed in in evidence the plaintiff's case closed.

Mr. Carton, Q.C., in opening the case for the defendants, said that the defendants commenced business as distillers in 1873. It was indisputable that the Whisky of Messrs. John Jameson and Son was the best Whisky. That was attributed by some to one thing, and by others to other things. Up to the present time the secret of the superior quality had not been discovered. But men casting about for the reason attributed it some to the water used by him, others to the quality of the grain that he used. The Dublin Distillery Company, on commencing business, determined to take John Jameson as their model, and at great expense they determined to have the water from the same level on the Royal Canal as that from which Messrs. John Jameson and Son, and they alone, got their water. They also determined that they would use nothing but the best native grain. In 1877 Messrs. Roe announced their price, not in the usual way, which is a definite announcement, but merely stating that "for the present" the price would be the same as it had been in the previous season. The Dublin Whisky Distillery Company, in 1876, finding the prices of native barley had increased greatly, were obliged to raise the prices, and the circular they had issued was necessary to justify this increase of price to their customers. Mr. Roe told them that in round numbers about 100,000 barrels of foreign barley were used in his establishment, and that they might take it for granted an enormous quantity of foreign barley was used in the manufacture. Another statement the defendants had undertaken to prove was that foreign barley was much cheaper to use in the manufacture than native grain. Mr. Roe purchased this enormous quantity of foreign barley at from 17s. 6d. to £1. During that month of October the average price of home-grown barley was 21s. 3d. If the defendants, therefore, had simply stated that old still Whisky could not be manufactured at last season's prices, unless from foreign barley, they would have been perfectly justified, and it would have been no libel upon Mr. Roe, or upon his trade. But did what they said in reference to damaged native grain necessarily refer to Mr. Roe? Counsel submitted that it did not fairly refer to Mr. Roe at all. They had heard from Mr. Norton that, during that season Irish barley was not good, that it was a wet season, and, as a matter of fact, there was a large amount of damaged native grain on the market. If the Dublin Distillery Company, while obeying the letter of their resolution to use nothing but native grain, had evaded the spirit of it by going in for damaged native grain, they would have been able to supply their customers with Whisky at the prices of last season. Counsel confidently put to the jury the issue that, in commenting upon the fact that there was damaged native grain in the market, it was never intended to mean that Mr. Roe used damaged grain in the manufacture of his Whisky.

Chief Justice Morris: That is not the issue—what they intended—it is what would be understood by anybody else reading it.

Mr. Carton: The construction of the document, of course, will help the jury.

Chief Justice Morris: If the writer has a loose meaning of his own he must suffer for it.

Mr. Carton said it would be for the jury to say whether the circular did any more that point out that Whisky could have been made at last season's price from foreign barley or from damaged native grain. Counsel then applied himself to the plea of privileged communication as to all but the words "or from damaged native grain." That plea was simply this: they had ascertained that Mr. Roe had issued this new price while the native barleys which they were using had gone up in price, and were likely to go higher, and it became necessary to explain to their customers why it was that they were increasing their price. They had heard, and believed, that Mr. Roe had bought large quantities of foreign barley, which he intended to use in the manufacture, and they had an interest in communicating to their customers why they were obliged to raise their price, and why old still Whisky made from native grain of the best quality could not be made at the price of 1876, owing to the increase that had taken place in the price of native barley. In October, 1877, the average price of native barley was 21s. 3d., while in the same month the previous year it was only 19s 3d. per barrel. Counsel objected altogether to the defendants being held responsible for what took place in London. Mr. Godsell was their agent for selling their Whisky—he was not their agent for slandering Mr. Roe. Mr. Roe himself gave the best proof that he believed Mr. Godsell was personally liable for what he did by bringing an action against him personally for £10,000, and an English jury had awarded him 40s. The defendants had nothing to say to what Mr. Godsell did in London behind their backs. As to Mr. Roe sustaining any damage by this libel, what was the fact? Not a single order that was given had been cancelled, not a single gallon of Whisky sold had been returned, and Mr. Roe was obliged to admit that not only was every gallon he made in 1877 sold, but he would have sold half as much again if he had made it. He thought so little of it himself that he had allowed twelve months to pass before bringing this action, and neither in his character nor in his high mercantile position had he suffered one jot of damage. It would be proved that this sample was not voluntarily sent to London at all, but was sent by Mr. Godsell's express request. Counsel was instructed that the distillation of this particular "period" from which the sample was taken was not of Mr. Roe's best make, and they would produce an eminent merchant of this city who bought a large quantity of this "period" and did not find it good or perfect Whisky. Undoubtedly the sample the Dublin Distillery Company got was a sample of musty Whisky. Under these circumstances Counsel confidently asked the jury to say that this was no libel, and that so far as it contained any defamatory matter, it was not to be taken as imputing to Mr. Roe that he used damaged grain in the manufacture of his Whisky.

At the conclusion of counsel's address, the Court adjourned to the next morning.

SECOND DAY.—NOVEMBER 30.

EVIDENCE for the defence was entered into.

Mr. James Costello, managing director of the Dublin Whisky Distillery Company (Limited), examined by Mr. Porter, Q.C., gave evidence that it was cheaper to use foreign barley than grain of native growth. In October, 1877, the average price of native barley was 19s. 3d. per barrel. At the same time in 1877 the price was 21s. 3d. That would make as nearly as possible a difference of 3½d. per gallon in Whisky. The attention of the directors was drawn to Mr. Roe's announcement that he would supply his customers at the previous season's price. Witness made one draft of a circular in the first instance. One of his colleagues drafted another, and witness embodied the two in the circular which was after-wards agree to and published. Witness was certainly not influenced by any malice or personal feeling towards Mr. Roe —he had quite a contrary feeling towards Mr. Roe. He believed the statements in the circular to be true, and certainly had no intention of injuring Mr. Roe's business. Mr. Godsell was appointed as their London agent, and was anxious for a sample of the Whisky of the other distillers of Dublin to compare with theirs, and to satisfy himself as to the relative merit of the two, and of their own particularly. Roe's was the only sample of new Whisky that was in the market at the time, and that was why they sent on Roe's. The sample which witness got through Mr. Soul was got without any privacy, and was, as far as witness knew, a perfectly genuine sample of Roe's Whisky. The directors smelled the sample, and said there was some peculiarity of smell about it, but they did not condemn it as witness had heard it condemned since. The whole trade knew that Mr. Roe was in the habit of using foreign barley. Witness never heard from anybody that Mr. Roe used damaged grain.

Mr. Porter: Did you mean to impute to Mr. Roe that he did use it?

Mr. Murphy, Q.C., objected, and the question was dis-allowed.

Mr. Porter: Having read the circular, in your opinion, is it the fair meaning of that circular that Mr. Roe had offered, or intended to offer for sale as Whisky made from native grain of the best quality Whisky which was made of damaged barley? Certainly not. Witness denied that the circular would bear that interpretation put upon it by any of the in-uendoes. The directors of the company were Messrs. Chamberlain, Malone, Alexander, Allen, Maturin, and witness.

Cross-examined by Mr. Murphy: Mr. Chamberlain is not a large holder of Roe's Whisky, Mr. Malone is one of the largest holders of Roe's Whisky in Dublin. Mr. Malone was at the meeting when the sample was examined. Witness was not a practical distiller nor maltster. 481 barrels of foreign barley were used by the Distillery Company. Witness overlooked these when he said in London that they never used foreign barley. He thought the 400 barrels were used without his being aware of it.

How did you first ascertain Mr. Roe's price? It was an-nounced in the papers. I did not see Mr. Grady on the day

B

before it was announced, and did not learn of it before I saw it in the newspapers.

Did Mr. Malone's draft circular contain the words "damaged grain"? I could not exactly recollect the precise words, but it certainly referred to inferior or damaged grain in the market. My own draft did not contain the words "damaged grain."

Did you show the draft to any solicitor?—No; no solicitor ever saw the draft before it was issued. I did not ask Mr. Malone for a sample, because I knew he had none of the new Whisky of that "period." I did not taste the Whisky nor smell it, not being a judge.

By the Chief Justice: I think the directors said there was a slight smell of must from it.

By Mr. Murphy: What was the difference of Roe's and your prices? They would come out about the same for small quantities.

What you mean is that it would be exactly the same?—That is so? If Mr. Roe supplies Whisky in casks of his own he would charge a higher price than we—a penny or twopence a gallon. In cases where parties supplied their own casks it would come out precisely the same. For large quantities we would be a penny less.

Chief Justice Morris: I thought up to this moment that Roe's was to be cheaper than yours, and that that was why you wanted to excuse yourselves.

Witness: We were under Mr. Roe the previous year, and our customers came to us and said, "Why are you raising your price in the face of Mr. Roe not raising his?" and that was the reason we found it necessary to go into this explanation.

By Mr. Porter: For sales of large quantities we were still under Mr. Roe, because we allowed a penny off for the casks.

Mr. Valentine Grady, an employé in the offices of the Company, deposed to having been asked by Mr. Soul, the secretary of the Company, to get a sample of Roe's Whisky; that he got it from Mr. Reynolds, and that he gave it to Mr. Soul precisely in the same condition as he received it.

Cross-examined by Mr. Atkinson: Some time afterwards he was directed to ask Mr. Reynolds for a sample exactly similar— not merely for a sample of Roe's Whisky.

Lawrence Malone, one of the directors of the defendants' Company, in reply to Mr. Monroe, Q.C., deposed that he was one of the directors who took part in the discussion as to the raising of the price of the Company. The price was raised in consequence of the increase of the price of the materials they used—the best native grain. Witness had formed, from the inquiries he had made of experts, an opinion as to whether the native or foreign grain is the best for the manufacture of Whisky.

Chief Justice Morris: I have formed an opinion about it myself, and I shall leave nobody in doubt as to what that opinion is (laughter).

By Mr. Monroe: The sample of Roe's Whisky on the Board table was on that day not considered as good as other "periods" of Roe's. There was something peculiar about it—something wild.

Chief Justice Morris: Something what?

Witness: Something wild.

Chief Justice Morris: I thought it might be something mild (laughter). Is "wild" a technical term which, translated into ordinary English, means "musty"?

Witness: It does not.

To Mr. Malone, Q.C.: Witness was not able to tell what "wildness" arises from. Witness though that in the fair meaning of the circular it did not impute that Mr. Roe was using damaged grain. In taking part in the discussion as to the circular witness was certainly not instigated by any malice towards Mr. Roe. Witness was himself a considerable purchaser of Mr. Roe's Whisky.

Cross-examined by Mr. Murphy, Q.C.: Witness bought some of Roe's Whisky in November. The quantity he bought was only a cask for the express purpose of sampling.

You bought a cask in order that you might form a clear opinion of it?—I had formed a clear opinion of it before from samples I had seen. I got one from Mr. Roe's stores. It was precisely the same as the other sample. I tasted it, and gave back nearly the entire of it to Mr. Stafford, in order to take it to another gentleman in town.

To Chief Justice Morris: Mr. Stafford is in the Whisky trade.

By Mr. Murphy: The quarter-cask—was that wild and musty, too?—It was precisely the same. I bought no more of that "period," but later in the season I bought a quantity in the market, not direct from Messrs. Roe. At the Board meeting an opinion was expressed, I believe, by Mr. Chamberlain, Mr. Allen, and myself, that the sample of Roe's Whisky on the table was inferior. I think the words "damaged grain" were not in the draft of the circular I made.

Chief Justice Morris: Did you hear Mr. Costello say it was not in his copy, and you say it was not in yours. How did it get into the circular?—It seems a problem to me.

Mr. Murphy, Q.C.: It got in in the distillation, my lord (laughter).

By Mr. Monroe, Q.C.: You say that the words "damaged grain" were not in your draft—was the expression "inferior grain" in it?—I think so. I think I used the words "inferior grain." The Whisky of Roe's make I bought afterwards did not possess the same characteristics.

Mr. Wm. Allen, another director of the Company, deposed, in reply to Mr. Porter, that in his opinion, but he could not speak as an expert, native barley was better than foreign for making Whisky.

Mr. Mathew Chamberlain, also a director of the Company, deposed that in using the words "damaged native grain" they were not intended to refer to Mr. Roe at all.

Cross-examined by Mr. Heron, Q.C.: Did you in using the words "foreign barley" mean to imply that Mr. Roe was making old still Whisky from foreign barley?—No; I did not mean to refer to Mr. Roe at all. The drafts before the Board on the 22nd had not the words "damaged grain." I should say that Whisky made from damaged grain would have a musty smell.

By Chief Justice Morris: You said that in neither of the drafts—neither Mr. Costello's nor Mr. Malone's—was there any reference to damaged grain?—No.

When on the 29th you saw that the words "damaged grain" had been introduced was there any reference to it then—to these words?—I don't think there was.

Was the printed proof read out?—It was.

Did any one call attention to why these words were introduced?—I believe not.

Mr. George Alexander, also a director of the Dublin Whisky Distillery Company, deposed to the Whisky having been examined at the meeting of the Board, and the statement being made that there was something peculiar about it, and that it was not up to Roe's usual make.

Cross-examined by Mr. Murphy, Q.C.: Do you recollect the phrase "musty" being used?—Yes.

And that it was not up to Roe's usual make?—Oh, no.

Were his prices discussed that day?—I forget whether it was that day or the day afterwards.

In the circular had you any intention of referring to Mr. Roe?—No.

Chief Justice Morris: Don't you know he was referred to as "one of our Dublin distillers" in the circular?

Witness: There was no reference to him personally.

Chief Justice Morris: The allegation is not that you referred to him in his personal capacity, but as George Roe and Co., distiller.

Witness: We did not mean it to apply except to our prices, and to the necessity we were under for raising our prices.

Chief Justice Morris: Well, I am afraid you were. That will do.

John Brannick, the Dublin Whisky Distillery Company's distiller, deposed that he had occupied that position since the formation of the Company, having been previously a short time in Mr. Roe's. The Company used the best grain that could be got—all native grain, with the exception of a trifle. The difference in the cost of native grain as compared with the previous season was about 2s. 3d. per barrel. That would make a difference in the price of Whisky of about 3d. or 3½d. a gallon.

Cross-examined by Mr. Heron, Q.C.: Witness did not try the sample said to be Roe's Whisky. While witness was in Mr. Roe's distillery they made first-class Whisky. Witness, had he been asked by the directors, could at once have told that the sample was not up to Roe's standard. Witness would not put his opinion as against that of Mr. Malone or Mr. Allen.

Mr. Carton, Q.C.: Is not Mr. Allen one of the best judges in Ireland of Whisky? I won't say that (laughter).

Mr. Heron: The best in Ireland is too strong; he won't swallow that as he would the sample (laughter).

To Chief Justice Morris: I am not aware whether it was the habit of the Board to test other people's Whisky.

Mr. Soul was recalled and stated that he handed the sample to Mr. Costello precisely in the same state in which he got it from Mr. Grady, with the exception that a small drop was taken out of it.

By a Juror: Why was the sample brought before the Board if it was for Mr. Godsell?—I did not know it was for Mr. Godsell at the time; I did not know for whom it was.

By Chief Justice Morris: Was it you that gave the draft of this circular to Mr. Wogan?—Yes.

Did you give it in the same condition you got it in from Mr. Costello?—I copied it out exactly the same.

Mr. Costello, recalled, at the request of his lordship.

By Chief Justice Morris: You stated in your examination that these words "damaged grain" were not in the draft? —Yes.

Mr. Malone has sworn they were in his draft?—Yes.

Mr. Soul swears that they were in the draft that you handed him—how do you account for that?—I account for it in this way: Mr. Malone had a reference in his circular to inferior native grain, and it was the wish of the Board to have something of the kind put into the circular. Then I incorporated that reference to native grain in the draft circular that was subsequently produced, and as far as I can recollect now in fixing the draft that was subsequently produced the word "damaged" was introduced instead "of inferior." I cannot say at whose suggestion—which member of the Board —it was introduced.

That was at the meeting of the Board where the sample was? —Not at all.

When?—Before the sample was produced.

Who was the gentleman that proposed that the word should be "damaged" instead of "inferior?"—I could not say who it was.

On what day?—It was at a special meeting that was held for the convenience of the directors in town. There is no record of it in the books. I think it was an informal meeting to fix this circular.

In whose office was it held?—I can't recollect whether it was in Mr. Malone's office or in Mr. Allen's.

Was the entire body of the directors there when this serious charge was made?—I think so.

Who were present?—I think Mr. Alexander; I am not quite sure Mr. Alexander was present.

Then if you are not, don't book him for it.

Mr. Chamberlain and Mr. Malone: I can't recollect whether Mr. Allen was present.

You can surely remember in whose office this informal meeting, of which there is no record, was held—it was not an everyday occurrence?—I can't. Frequently we met in the offices of one or other of the directors, sometimes Mr. Malone's, sometimes in Mr. Allen's, and sometimes in Mr. Chamberlain's. I think it was in Mr. Malone's on this occasion.

What was the date of that?—It must have been two or three days before the issue of the circular.

The circular was issued on the 29th?—It is dated the 27th.

You said the date it was issued?—I can fix it only approximately.

Approximate it as near as you can?—I should say about the 26th.

Had you got the sample at that time?—No, my lord.

What day did you first see the sample?—I think it was the day it was sent on to Mr. Godsell.

Do you know that Mr. Soul had the sample on the 26th?— I was not aware. The first time I saw it was on the Board table.

Were there any other alterations made in this circular at this meeting of which you have no record?—No, my lord, I think nothing else—nothing else.

Was there any reference at the regular meeting of the directors on the 29th, to any alteration having been made in the circular at this informal meeting?—I think not.

Mr. Heron said a letter was in evidence showing that the circulars, complete, were sent to London on the 26th.

Mr. Stein, operative distiller for Messrs. Roe, was recalled, and in answer to Mr. Heron, said that the two first "periods" of the season of 1877 commenced, the first on the 4th October and ended on the 16th; the second on the 15th, and ended on the 26th. Both were uniform, and both were the best Dublin Whisky. If the first "period" had been foul or musty it would have been carried over to the second by the "feints," which are carried from one "period" to another.

Cross-examined by Mr. Porter, Q.C.: home and foreign barley were used—one-third foreign against two-thirds home.

Mr. Heron: Would any judge fine the trace——

Chief Justice Morris: Any judge of Whisky (laughter).

By Mr. Heron: Would any judge of Whisky detect a trace of "must?"—Most easily. We sometimes find the foreign grain to be the best. This year the Scotch is far better than the Irish.

Mr. Harris was recalled by Mr. Murphy, Q.C., for the plaintiff, and stated that the 47,500 gallons of the first "period," and the 53,000 gallons of the second "period" were all sold, and there were no complaints.

Mr. J. Stafford, wine and spirit merchant, was called on the part of the defendants', and stated that he procured from the store clerk at Roe's distillery a sample of Roe's new Whisky about the 23rd or 24th or October, and found it had a musty taste. Asked Mr. Malone to taste it, and gave portion of the sample to a Mr. Smith.

Cross-examined: Mr. Smith was the partner of a Mr. Menzies, who was the defendants' Company.

Mr. A. M. Porter, Q.C., summed up for the defendants.

Mr. Murphy, Q.C., replied for the plaintiff.

Chief Justice Morris, in putting the case to the jury, said, as they were aware, this was an action brought by the plaintiff, Mr. Henry Roe, who traded under the name of George Roe and Co., as many old firms carried on the old name, although the person who would answer to that name might have long since gone. He mentioned that because there was a quantity of matter addressed to them as if there was any allegation that the defendants had any personal malice to Mr. Henry Roe, who now carried on the firm. What the plaintiff really alleged was that they had malice to his business, and in that capacity he brought an action for libel on him in his business. The subject matter of this libel was a circular, which it appeared was issued by the defendants either through their managing director, Mr. Costello, or through their secretary, Mr. Soul—for it appeared that this Company, different from the common adage applied to all corporations and companies, had a *soul* (laughter)—on the 26th October, 1877, and which appeared to have reached the hands of a gentleman of the rather singular name of Godsell (laughter), who lived in London, but who had been listening to this trial, although it was stated he had been out in the square admiring the architecture (laughter). In consequence of the voluminous pleadings there would be seven questions for the jury. It was not his duty to interfere with the province of a jury, but he hoped they seldom had any doubt of what his opinion of a case was when he did form a strong opinion on one. Sometimes there was so much to be said on both sides that he was not sorry the responsibility of deciding between them lay with the jury. Sometimes a case appeared to him to be pretty plain, and this appeared to be one of that class. The first question was: Did the defendants publish the circular? Of that there could be no question. The second was: Was it published in any defamatory sense? Well, if it applied to the plaintiff, and if it suggested that the plaintiff was making Whisky either from damaged grain or in any other improper way, there could be no doubt it was published in a defamatory sense. Thirdly, was it published in the defamatory sense alleged in the second, third, fourth, and fifth paragraphs, or any of them? The paragraphs varied the sense a good deal. The fourth would appear to him to push it beyond what the words would legitimately suggest, for it said that the allegation was that Mr. Roe was doing this "fraudulently." The next question was: Was it published of the plaintiff in relation to his trade? If it was published of him at all it was in relation to his trade, for there was no allegation at all against him in his private or personal capacity. The next question was: Was the circular a libel? That was a question for the jury. If they could have no doubt that it did refer to Mr. Roe in his capacity of a trader, and if it suggested that he was making Whisky from this damaged grain in the way suggested, it would be for the jury

to say whether there could be a grosser libel. He could
scarcely conceive a grosser libel than if it was imputed that a
man who had inherited, after a period of one hundred years,
such a name and such a business, attempted, in order to
increase his gains slightly, to destroy his firm ,his credit, and
the article he was producing—if that was the allegation suggested; six and seven merely took defence to part of the libel,
leaving out the principal part, and one of them was threat the
libel was written *bona fide*, believing it to be true, and not
from malice, while the other was an actual justification that
it was true—all except the words "from damaged native
grain." It would appear to his lordship (and he would not be
beating about the bush with them) that the real and sustan-
tial question they would have to decide would be the amount
of damages. It appeared that Mr. Roe commenced this action
some time last year, and that he did not go on with it, and
that had been urged as a cause of complaint against him.
Why he did not go on with it his Lordship really did not know,
beyond this, that it had been developed in evidence that he
also had an action against this Mr. Godsell for what he had
done in London, and he had got a verdict against him for
40s, which was the amount that would have carried the costs
of the proceedings in London. What the defence of Godsell
was upon that occasion they did not know, but there were fifty
ways in which it might have been explained, for he might
have gone into the box and said he was an innocent poor
fellow, who was only the agent of the people who had sent
him over the sample, and why should he be mulcted: His
Lordship could not imagine an English counsel getting up and
saying, "Why mulct this poor English fellow here when the
real culprits are the Distillery Company over in Dublin?"
If they had this Godsell in the box instead of being outside
admiring the architecture, his Lordship at least intended to
have tried to find out whether he might not have made out
that he was an innocent poor agent, when the real culprits
were the persons who set him in motion, were the people who
sent him so many circulars that it took £2 10s. for postage.
It must have increased the revenue of the Post Office sub-
stantially that week (laughter), and who sent him over
this little bottle of Whisky? But now they had the real
parties before them who undoubtedly put this poor Godsell in
motion. He came over in October to be made an agent. He
had communications with Mr. Costello, who appeared to be
managing director of this Whisky Company, and who appeared

to be of a literary turn (laughter). In that respect, his co-director, Malone, whose palate for tasting Whisky his own distiller (Brannick) declared to be unequalled in Ireland, except by his own (laughter), appeared to have combined also a literary turn. It was a dangerous quality sometimes, and there was an old saying that everybody should stick to his own business—every cobbler to his last (laughter). That was a free translation of a sentence of Horace's, with which he would not trouble them further (laughter). Accordingly he thought it would have been better if Costello had kept on managing, and if Malone had kept on tasting (laughter), and they might have kept themselves out of the hobble they had brought their Company into by indulging their literary turn. One or two of their directors—they appeared to be all of the Whisky trade— were cross-examined as to their knowledge of this circular. One of them—an elderly and rather dull, but, his lordship had no doubt a most respectable old gentleman (laughter)—appeared to have ignored at once the idea of his writing a circular. It appeared that Costello and Malone, the real culprits, if culprits they were, were not satisfied until Costello wrote his own draft and Malone applied his own unassisted intellect to write another (laughter), and then they clubbed the two together, and for a long time his lordship was under the impression that out of a combination of the two drafts came the circular in question, but it now appeared it did not. Some of the gentlemen never saw it after seeing the drafts until they saw it in print, and one intelligent and respectable gentleman, named Chamberlain, appeared to be rather puzzled and dissatisfied how the words "damaged native grain" got into the circular, for when the combined draft was before the Board on the 20th October, he did not think the words were in it. But it appeared what was called an "informal meeting"—that is, a meeting together of Costello and somebody else in Malone's Whisky store (laughter), instead of in the meeting-room of the Company, was held, and this circular was what was called "heel-tapped" (laughter), because on that occasion was introduced what the plaintiff thought the most damaging accusation against him—namely, the use of the words "damaged native grain." Having drawn up this circular, they issued it, apparently without bringing it before the Board again. His lordship was greatly struck with the introduction of the words "damaged native grain." He could not for a long time see why it was changed from the word "inferior" grain, which Malone used in his calmer moment when drawing up this wonderful effort of his; but it had now developed itself on the evidence that Stafford, the dark-haired young man, who had been called the little shareholder—his lordship did not know whether arising from his stature or from his poverty of shares (laughter)—Stafford had taken Malone into council, hearing that he was the greatest taster in Ireland except Brannick, the distiller—to taste a little sample that he had already got of this Whisky of Roe's, which occurrence, he said, took place about the 23rd or 24th of October. Now, the circular, without the words "damaged native grain" at all in it, had passed the Board on the 20th. There was some reference to inferior grain, which Costello, as a literary man, considered a synonymous term with damaged. His lordship yielded to no man in ignorance of distilling (laughter), but he should say there was a very substantial difference between the two. Inferior grain might not give the very best flavour, but would not do the Whisky any positive harm, whereas there was nothing in the world that would give Whisky a musty flavour more than damaged grain. His lordship observed a most mar-vellous dislike of all the co-defendants using the word "musty." He had to assist them several times (laughter). They boggled at that word "musty," and it struck him at once, because musty Whisky, it appeared upon the evidence, was exactly what would be the production of damaged grain. It was an odd thing, to say the least of it, that just about the time that by the evidence Malone would have got from the little shareholder the sample which had a musty flavour, the circular, which had passed the Board, and which had already combined the literary effusions of Malone and Costello, was altered at the twelfth hour by the introduction of the words "damaged grain," which, they saw now, was a very unpleasant thing, because it exactly answered the sample of Roe's Whisky, and because, if he had produced musty Whisky, he would have been likely to have used damaged grain. What took place then? On the 26th all these circulars were sent over to Godsell; whether it was that the letter-carriers were weighed down with the number of them, he did not know, but it appeared that they were not delivered finally till the 30th October. When Godsell got them he dis-seminated them all over the country, addressed to the customers of Mr. Roe, because a Mr. Figgins, a gentleman from England —he believed that was his name—

Mr. Murphy: Figgis, my lord.

Chief Justice Morris: One name is as good as the other—there is not a fig between them, at all events (laughter). Mr. Figgis told them that he got one of the circulars from a customer of Mr. Roe's in Liverpool, a gentleman who had ordered 600 puncheons, which, at £22 a puncheon, would amount to some £13,000 or £14,000. That circular was not, at

all events, likely to make him increase his order (laughter), and
they might be sure he sent it to Mr. Figgis, not for the purpose of seeing whether the spelling was according to the
phonetic system (laughter). Then a gentleman named Sutton,
an English gentleman, and a good man of business, told them
how Godsell waited upon him and introduced this sample of
Roe's Whisky, and how they came to the conclusion that it was
made from damaged corn. Was not that a very cautious thing?
They actually arrived at the very same conclusion that appeared
in the circular—that it must have been made from damaged corn;
and then Mr. Sutton, who had ordered 100 puncheons, countermanded his order for the time. However, upon finding out
that there was nothing really wrong with the Whisky, he con-
firmed his order. Of course there was no loss to Mr. Roe, but
whose fault was that? There had been a good deal of allegation on the part of the defendants that Mr. Roe had suffered
no loss. That was no answer at all. If they libelled a man,
and that his personal character was so good that it did him no
harm, it was no answer to say, "Well, I libelled you but you
are such a tremendously honest fellow that nobody believed
me" (laughter). That appeared to be practically the sort of
defence raised on that point. Come to read the thing itself,
with the light which they were entitled to use from the surrounding circumstances at the time, it was quite clear that the
representatives of the defendants here were dissatisfied that
Mr. Roe did not raise his price for Whisky. It appeared that
his price was still a penny a gallon over theirs when they did
raise the price, and a profit of a penny a gallon upon 2,000,000
gallons would be £8,500; so that he would have all the profit
that they would have plus £8,500; and he could quite understand distillers of great name not raising their prices, though
for that particular year they might not make as much as in
other years, especially if they made advantageous contracts.
They evidently were dissatisfied with that. Grady, who
combined the useful occupation of town traveller and collector
with the position of a writer in the *Freeman's Journal*—revolu-
tionising the money market of the world, he had not doubt—
told them that, having got hold of this quotation of Roe's, he
wrote some comments on it in the *Freeman's Journal*. These
were seen by the directors on the morning of the 15th, and they
evidently were dissatisfied, because their customers were asking
why they were raising their own price. His lordship should
have thought the ready answer was, "Roe is a great deal above
us, and we will be still under him." But they cast about for a
sample of Roe's Whisky. He did not understand that it was
imputed by Mr. Heron that this sample was fabricated by the

defendants. All that was said was that it was a queer sort of business, and that as the sample was musty the way in which it was got hold of was muddy, for, instead of apply- ing direct for it to Roe, if they wanted to challenge his make, they went a roundabout way of obtaining it, and sent it over to Godsell, who went about to Roe's customers, saying, "Look here, Roe wants 4s. a gallon for Whisky made from damaged grain, and I am giving you for 3s. 11d. a drink that is just as good as John Jameson's, for it is made from the same canal" (laughter). That was the view Sutton took of it, for when he found the article was musty, he countermanded the order for the time. That was what Mr. Allingham and Mr. Devine thought to be the point of the circular. Mr. Harris said many customers of Roe's came to the distillery, several of them wanting samples, who had previously bought by the brand. A great many dull men like Allingham, who confined himself to the Whisky business, and had not an intellectual turn like Malone (laughter), thought the circular referred to Roe, and it was the talk of the world the jury must deal with, not with some professor who might read the words by the aid of theological casuistry. The question was what a plain, ordi- nary sort of man would understand by it. Godsell had no doubt at all what it meant. The circular first made the abstract statement that a distiller in Dublin (who no doubt was Mr. Roe) would not raise his price—that they were obliged to raise it because they used good grain. "This begins a new paragraph," says Mr. Porter. "It is in the disjunctive," said his colleague—as if all the Whisky-buyers reading the circular were going about with Lindley Murray under their arms (laughter). It was a new paragraph, but beginning in a very queer way— "No doubt;" that was a phrase that rather connected it with the previous sentence. "No doubt old still Whisky could be made"—the suggestion was that this was a mere abstract state- ment, such a piece of information as they would see in the new "Encyclopædia Britannica" under the letter W (laughter)— "No doubt old still whisky could be made from foreign barley or from damaged native grain at the prices of last season, or even less." Had the jury any doubt that that was meant to apply to Roe? Was there not a defence on the file saying that it did apply to him except as to the damaged grain, and justify- ing it because he did use foreign barley? But because it was in the disjunctive they were to drop Roe there at "foreign," and Allingham, the Whisky-buyer in Capel Street, was up to the conjunctive, and would know at once that he should drop Roe there and put in some unknown dark horse that nobody ever heard of (laughter). It was said that the defendants were not taken in with the four distillers called "the four-in-hand" in some treatise that had been referred to. They knew there was some gentleman named O'Sullivan, a member of Parliament, who was continually protesting against their mixing Dublin Whisky with this stuff called silent Whisky, which appeared to be of a very bad character, his Lordship believed— he did not know (laughter). It was said Mr. Roe and his comrades of the four-in-hand rather threw cold water on provincial-made Whisky, and said it might be called Whisky, and that that was all that could be said for it; however, he presumed, if provincial distillers were dissatisfied with anything in that pamphlet, they would be able to take care of themselves. The defendants, carried away by anger at finding that Mr. Roe was not raising his price, appeared to have cast about to disparage his make. The jury must have very little doubt now, at all events, what his Lordship thought upon the whole case. It was not a case for giving very large damages, because Mr. Roe had not, as a matter of fact, suffered any positive injury. On the other hand, if the jury were to give nominal damages, it might be said, as it often was, "Oh, you got a great sum, did you not?" and it might be said they very nearly proved their case. Let the jury not suppose he wished them to follow his opinion, except so far that he tried a good many of these cases, and he generally saw how the land lay (laughter)—at all events, he would make a very good thirteenth juror if he was put into the box (laughter). The jury would exercise their good judgment, and arrive at a solution which he hoped would be satisfactory to both parties (laughter).

The jury, after three-quarters of an hour's absence, found for the plaintiff—£100 damages.

Mr. Heron asked for the judgment for the plaintiff, which was granted.

GENUINE DUBLIN WHISKY.

THE MOST WHOLESOME OF ALL SPIRITS.

DUBLIN WHISKY distilled by Messrs. JOHN JAMESON & SON, WILLIAM JAMESON & CO., JOHN POWER & SON, and GEORGE ROE & CO., can be obtained in Wood by wholesale merchants and dealers, direct from their respective distilleries.

DUBLIN WHISKY.—Messrs. WILLIAM JAMESON & CO. and GEORGE ROE & CO. can also supply their Whiskies in cases, the bottles protected by capsule, label, and brand on corks.

Afterword

George Roe & Co. were deservedly upset by the allegations so poorly hinted at in the offending DWD circular. It might not have been entirely apparent to the common man or anyone without an intimate knowledge of the Dublin whisky trade, but closer inspection of the text certainly does bring out the implication that Roe & Co.—being the only Dublin distiller to have announced their (unchanged) prices for the coming season—was only able to do so with the use of suspect grain. Unsurprisingly, Roe & Co. made their objection to this insinuation public within a matter of days after publication. They demanded an apology from the Dublin Whisky Distilling Company (DWD) and received one really only regretting that offense was taken by Roe & Co. but not necessarily for making the accusation in the first place, veiled or direct. After a period where Roe & Co. considered dropping the matter, it was decided action must be taken to protect their century-plus long and hard-earned reputation to make sure that both the public and any industry concerns knew once and for all that the whisky produced by Roe's Thomas Street distillery was and always will be of the highest quality possible. Preparations were set in motion and nearly a year after the libelous offense, the case was filed against the DWD and the trial was set for late November which eventually resulted in the abbreviated transcript in this book.

The Dublin trial, as is mentioned in this transcript's Preface, was not the first action of a legal nature taken by George Roe & Co. in this matter. Since the circular in question made its public debut in London and was initially distributed by DWD's London agent, Fredrick

H. Godsell, London would also be the starting point of Roe's defense of their product and reputation. A case surrounding the slander and libel allegedly perpetrated by Mr. Godsell was filed and brought to trial in July of 1878. The following article that appeared in the August 1 issue of *The British Trade Journal* provides a fine summation of that trial and results:

ROE'S BRAND OF WHISKY IMPUGNED.

Roe *v.* Godsell was an action for libel and slander, heard in the Queen's Bench Division of the High Court of Justice, before Mr. Justice Field and a special jury.

The plaintiff carries on business in Dublin as a distiller of whisky under the style of "Roe & Co.," and the defendant is the London agent of the Dublin Whisky Distillery Company. It appeared from the evidence that the best whisky is called Old Still, and is made from the best barley only. By means of a patent still inferior whisky is made from damaged or inferior barley, and this is known in the trade as "silent whisky." It is a practice of the Dublin distillers to announce in October the price for the coming season, and the plaintiff, in 1877, named 4*s.* 1*d.* per gallon as that of his manufacture. The company had then caused a circular to be printed in Dublin, which contained the alleged libel, and copies of it were sent to their London agent, the defendant in this action, who gave or sent them to persons here interested in the trade. It was to the effect that the plaintiff was selling and offering for sale as Old Still whisky that which from the price could not have been made from the best grain only. It was further complained that the defendant had falsely and maliciously spoken the following words:—"The company can prove that Roe has bought and used in his distillery damaged grain. This (producing a sample bottle) is a sample of his new whisky." It appeared that the company had procured some of Roe's whisky, which had been sent as a sample to spirit merchants in Dublin, and which, for some unexplained reason, was faulty, having a decidedly musty flavour. The directors of the company know that it was not a fair sample of the ordinary merchantable article of Roe's manufacture when they sent it to the defendant, who stated that as soon as he tasted it he came to the conclusion that it had been made from grain which had "shot." He denied that he had ever used the words complained of, but on this pint there was a conflict of evidence. The publication of the circular was admitted, but it was contended that the statements in it concerning the plaintiff were not libelous and were written without malice; but it was not maintained that it was in any way privileged. The plaintiff contended that it was untrue, and that to the knowledge of the defendant, and that there was express malice in it. As to damages, it was not sought to recover any large sum, though 5,000*l*. had been originally claimed, nor was there any evidence of pecuniary loss.

The learned Judge in summing up told the jury it would be for them to say whether or not the defendant had accused Mr. Roe of using damaged grain, and also whether the plaintiff had made out to their satisfaction that in the circular he was disparaged in his business as a distiller. They would have to consider any indirect pecuniary loss to the plaintiff, if they found in his favour, and give him reasonable damages. Then, to, they should fully consider the motives of the defendant, and also whether or not he was actuated by a wish to disparage the plaintiff in the market.

The jury, after an hour's deliberation, found in favour of the plaintiff, with 40*s*. damages.

After Mr. Godsell was thoroughly drubbed in the London court, Dublin and the DWD itself were next. As you've by now read, George Roe & Co. very successfully defended their position and essentially exposed James Costello, the manager of the Dublin

Whisky Distilling Company, as the composer of the circular's final draft along with the assistance of George Soul, secretary at DWD. As Roe's actual financial losses were non-existent and their reputation was already so high as to render any accusations of impropriety irrelevant and unfounded, the jury made quick work of the verdict against the DWD which was accepted by the judge who seemed less and less impartial as the trial progressed. In his closing statements, Chief Justice Morris hinted at what the Dublin Whisky Distilling Company's motive might have been. Having only been founded in 1872 with production commencing in the Spring of 1873, DWD was the 'new kid on the block'. And even though they compared production-wise very closely to that of George Roe & Co. and the other three main Dublin distillers (John Jameson & Sons, Wm. Jameson & Co. and John Powers & Son), they were not yet accepted into that fraternity and were seen as an upstart or outsider distillery. They had not earned their place alongside the other respected and long-established traditional distilling houses. Continually comparing their product to Jameson's or Roe's, they longed to be included if for any other reason than the added prestige such a relationship would bring to their operations.

Also, the four Dublin distillers had just released the pamphlet, *Dublin Whisky, Genuine & Spurious* (a defense of Dublin whisky against whisky blending and the production of 'silent spirit' from Coffey stills), the DWD was not invited to join the others as a signatory partner. Nor were they invited to join in the presentation of *Truths About Whisky*, the more recognized work that expands on the controversies presented in *Dublin Whisky, Genuine & Spurious*.

Animosity at their industrial snubbing may have been a primary yet subversive reason behind the need felt to release a statement that justified the virtues of their efforts while impugning the efforts of others in such a loosely intended fashion.

Even though it was made clear that the DWD was entirely at fault for this transgression, they were able to save face and gain some positives from their litigious loss. The advertisement at the end of this Afterword appeared in many publications throughout Great Britain – the example here is from *Thom's Official Directory of the United Kingdom of Great Britain and Ireland*, 1883, Alexander Thom & Co. – in which three points established in the 1878 trial are proudly listed concerning their water source (same as Jameson's), native barley being best-suited for Whisky production and that DWD's production process matches the industry's best.

In the end, the competing Dublin distilleries were forced to put aside their differences and unite in an effort to bolster the stability of traditional Dublin whisky production. The continued rise of blends and the inclusion of 'silent spirit' as a whisky and it's place in the new blending industry continually weakened the profile of Dublin whisky as the distillers held steadfast to their traditional ways and made no acceptance of the changes sweeping through the whisky industry. In 1891, the Dublin Whisky Distilling Company joined forces with William Jameson & Co. and their former accuser, George Roe & Co. to form the Dublin Distillers' Company, Ltd. This association was troubled from the start as the initial investment cost was considered to be over-valued for the industry and companies involved. Also, after the distilleries were brought under this banner, they were still allowed to compete against each other for sales and market share across their combined territories. Eventually, all three distilleries under the Dublin Distillers' Company, Ltd. banner would meet permanent closure by the early 1920's.

In 2017, (George) Roe & Co.'s name would be welcomed back as a premium Irish whiskey presented by Diageo (to whom this book has no relation).

Other works from
Aaron Barker Publishing

The Whisky Distilleries of the United Kingdom
Alfred Barnard

British and Foreign Spirits
Charles Tovey

A Ramble Through Classic Canongate
Alfred Barnard

Condensing and Cooling in Pot-Still and
Patent-Still Distillation
J.A. Nettleton

A Visit to Watson's Dundee Whisky Stores
(with discussion about the 1906 Dundee Whisky Fire, other
whisky fires and the operations of John Robertson & Son)
Alfred Barnard

The History of a Great House
John Jameson & Harry Clarke

Dublin Whisky, Genuine and Spurious
John Jameson, et al.

Dublin Whisky, Report of the Late Trial,
Roe v. The Dublin Whisky Distillery Co.
George Roe & Co.

(coming in 2017 or after)
Joseph Scarisbrick's Revenue Series.
Beer Manual: History and Technical
Spirit Manual: History and Technical
Hydrometry and Spirit Values

DUBLIN WHISKY,

REPORT OF THE LATE TRIAL.

ROE

v.

THE DUBLIN WHISKY DISTILLERY COMPANY, LIMITED.

[1878]

2017 EDITION
Copyright © Layout and Afterword
AARON BARKER PUBLISHING
Carmel, Indiana
whiskywheels@gmail.com
ISBN: 978-0-9909072-9-9

Read your Whisky.